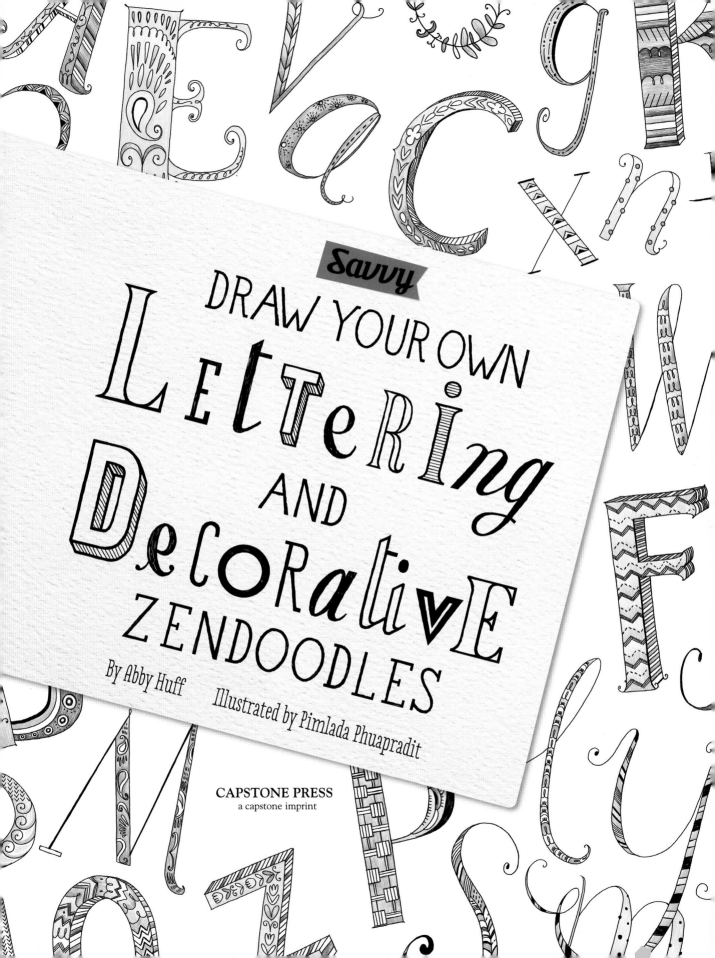

Savvy

DRAW YOUR OWN
LETTERING
AND
DECORATIVE
ZENDOODLES

By Abby Huff   Illustrated by Pimlada Phuapradit

CAPSTONE PRESS
a capstone imprint

Savvy Books are published by Capstone Press, a Capstone imprint
1710 Roe Crest Drive
North Mankato, Minnesota 56003
www.mycapstone.com

Library of Congress Cataloging-in-Publication Data
Names: Huff, Abby, 1991– author. | Phuapradit, Pimlada, illustrator.
Title: Draw your own lettering and decorative zendoodles / by Abby Huff ;
   illustrated by Pimlada Phuapradit.
Description: North Mankato, Minnesota : Capstone, 2017. | Series: Savvy.
   Draw your own zendoodles | Audience: Ages 9–13. | Audience: Grades 4 to 8.
Identifiers: LCCN 2016044396 | ISBN 9781515748410 (library binding) |
   ISBN 9781515748489 (ebook pdf)
Subjects: LCSH: Lettering—Technique—Juvenile literature. | Decoration and
   ornament—Juvenile literature. | Handicraft for children—Juvenile literature.
Classification: LCC NK3600 .H84 2017 | DDC 745.6/1—dc23
LC record available at https://lccn.loc.gov/2016044396

Editorial Credits
Bobbie Nuytten, designer; Jo Miller, media researcher; Laura Manthe, premedia specialist

Image Credits
Capstone Studio: Karon Dubke, 7 (all), 44-47 (all), Shutterstock: Aleks Melnik, 30 (watercolor), bigjom
jom, 19, DONOY6_STUDIO, 37, gresei, 12, J. Helgason, 14, lightofchairat, 16, LiliGraphie, 40, Zadorozhnyi
Viktor, 30 (brush); Backgrounds: Shutterstock: aopsan, arigato, CCat82, donatas1205, happykanppy, Lana
Veshta, macknimal, Mikhail Pogosov, Nik Merkulov, Only background, Piotr Zajc, Ratana21, redstone,
siriak kaewgorn, Turbojet, Vadim Georgiev

Crafts created by Lori Blackwell and Tyson J. Schultz

Printed in the United States of America.
010062S17

Table of Contents

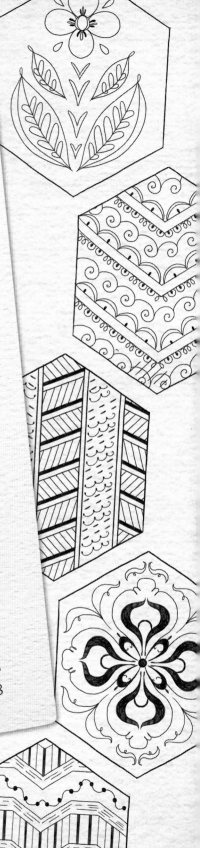

Zendoodle Basics

Need to de-stress? Flip open your sketchbook and start drawing zendoodles! A zendoodle is an extravagant design built up from easy patterns. It's also a perfect way to unwind and get creative. Don't sweat getting zendoodles just right — always go with whatever feels best to *you*. Enjoy the process and let your pencil flow across the page. Get started with a few fundamentals and begin your artistic adventure!

Patterns

Zendoodles may look complicated, but they're created from basic patterns. Make patterns by repeating and layering different strokes and shapes. Using multiple designs in a zendoodle gives it its signature tangled style.

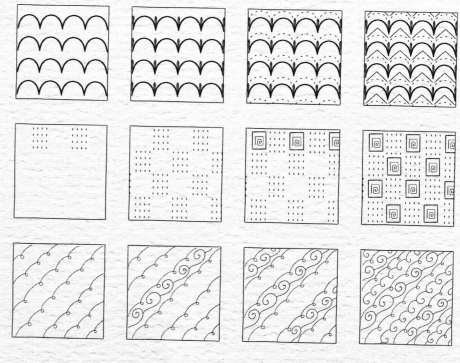

Shapes and Motifs

Small shapes and motifs (a fancy word for reoccurring forms and elements) can be used to help fill a zendoodle. Use teardrops, fans, circles, flowers, and more. Try drawing a cluster of shapes in your zendoodle or spread them out. Decorate them with dots, lines, or a pattern for an elaborate look.

Adding Patterns

Adding patterns is the most fun and relaxing part of
the zendoodle process. There are two main methods.
Try both to see which you like best.

Sectioned
Divide your drawing with lines.
Fill each section with a pattern.

Free-formed
Let your patterns overlap and run into
each other. When you're done, it should
be hard to tell where one pattern begins
and another ends.

Object Zendoodles

Zendoodles don't have to resemble anything. You can simply fill a page with intricate designs. Other times, it's fun to make your zendoodle into a recognizable object, like a cloud or letter. When you're working with an object, try experimenting with these two methods.

Positive space
Draw inside the object. This is using the positive space — the space occupied by a subject. Decorate within the lines using adorable details and doodles.

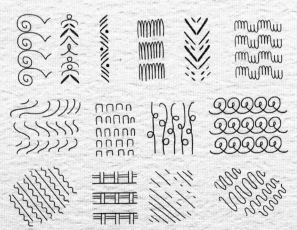

Negative space
Draw around the object. This is using the negative space — the space around a subject. For maximum impact, don't add any details inside the object. Leave it completely blank for a striking graphic look.

Warm Up

Loosen your wrist and relax your mind. Get started with zigzags, squiggles, dots, curls, and more.

Zendoodle Tools & Materials

If you have a pencil and a scrap of paper, you're ready to zendoodle! But it can be fun to try out other supplies too. Here are a few essentials to keep in your toolbox.

Pencils

The most basic doodle tool. Try a mechanical pencil for consistently precise, even lines.

Paper

A page from your notebook can do in a pinch. For best results, use drawing or sketch paper. The thicker paper will hold up better to erasing and marking. Paper also comes in different textures. Generally, it'll be easier to doodle on a smooth surface.

Pens

Pens are perfect for polished zendoodles. Splurge on drawing pens for smoother, high quality lines. Look for archival or pigment ink pens. The special ink won't smudge or fade, so it'll keep your design looking pretty.

Colors

Zendoodles are bold in black and white, but color adds a whole new dimension. Use colored pencils for a soft look. Try markers and colored pens for dramatic color. There are many options to choose from. Enjoy experimenting!

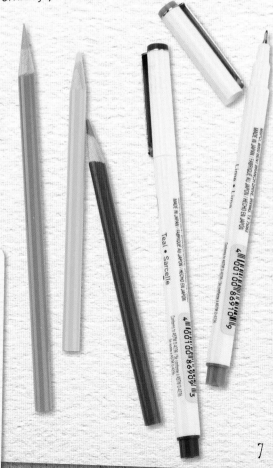

Quick and Easy Zendoodles

Not feeling confident in your drawing abilities? Want to start doodling right away? Head to **capstonekids.com**. There you can download sheets with blank outlines. Simply print the page and you're ready to go. Add exciting patterns and designs to make it your own.

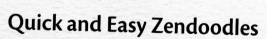

Expressive Borders

Basic doesn't have to be boring. Borders are perfect for adding a little zendoodle flair to any page. Go geometric, natural, curly, or funky. Try stacking multiple frames on top of each other for a chunky, elaborate decoration.

Start simple

Add more as you go

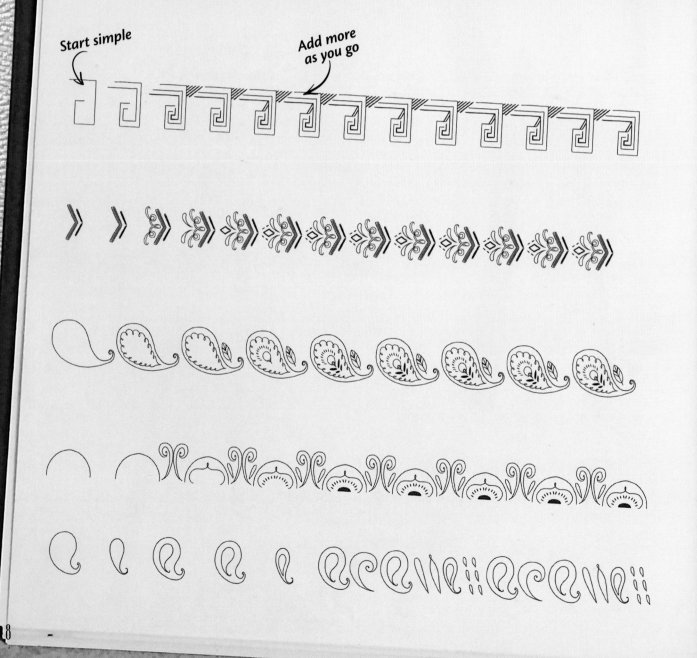

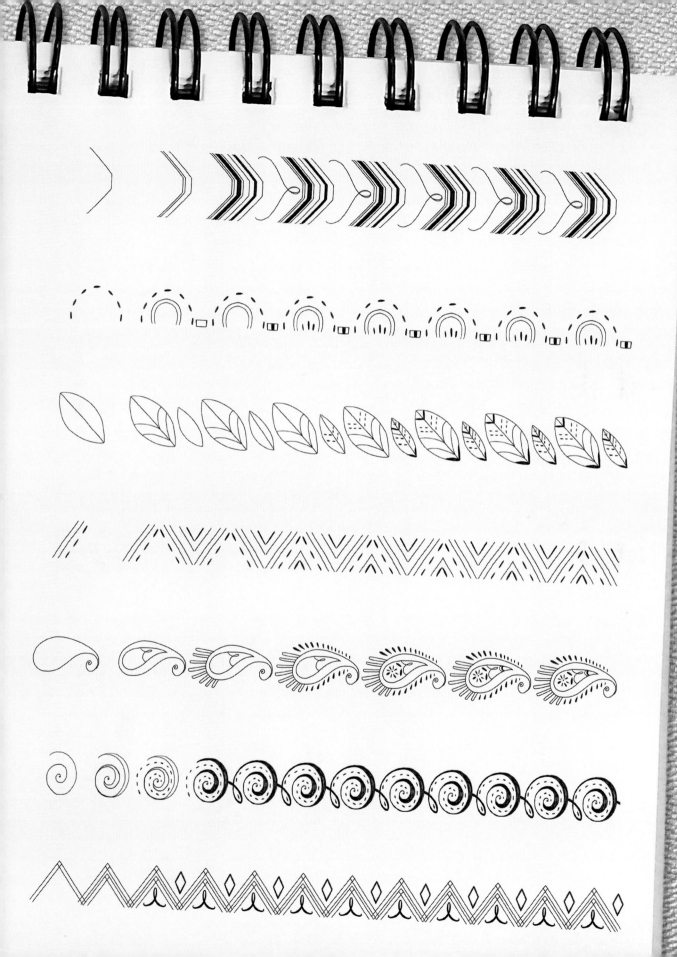

9

Corner Clusters

A doodle forever favorite! Corner zendoodles make a great finishing touch for hand-drawn designs. Draw mini border patterns or build up your doodle using curvy shapes, flowers, and other elements. Keep the cluster small and simple or let it grow and grow. Relax and just go with the flow!

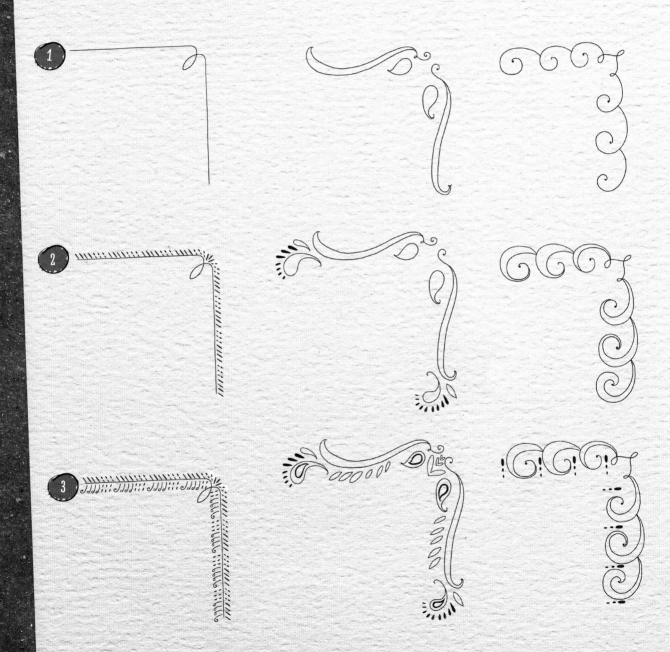

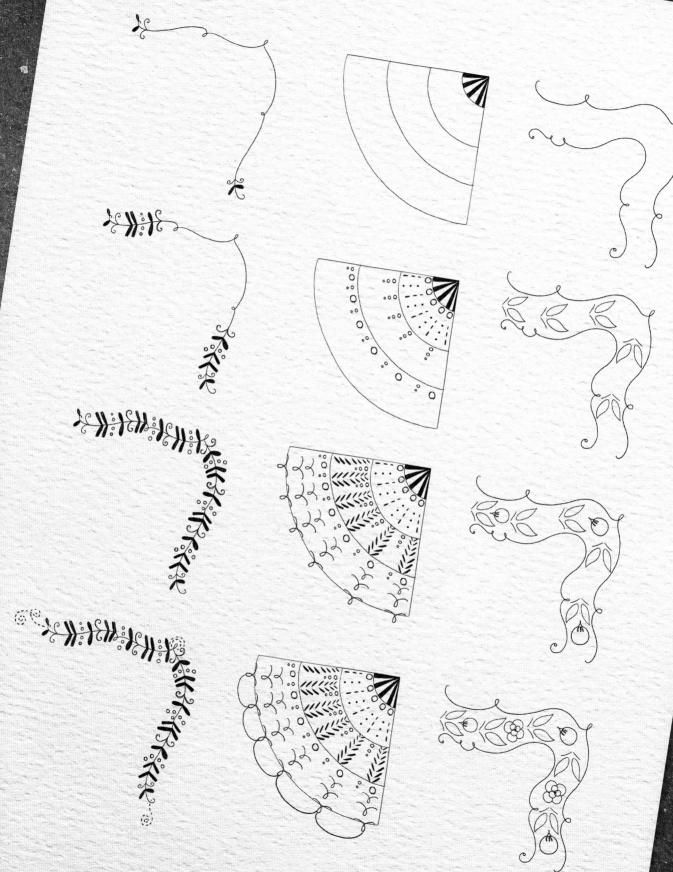

Color It!

Turn your zendoodles into custom coloring pages. If you drew in pencil, trace over your design with black pen. A waterproof or archival quality pen is best. The ink won't bleed if you color over it. Now you're ready to start coloring with your favorite tool. Or, before you color, make photocopies of your zendoodle. That way you can color it again and again. You could even host a coloring party for you and your friends!

Pretty Pattern Tiles

Practice your patterns in the cutest way possible. Start by covering your page with hexagons. Fill the honeycomb of tiles with sweet doodles and flower motifs. If hexagons aren't your style, try other shapes. Circles, squares, and triangles are all great options.

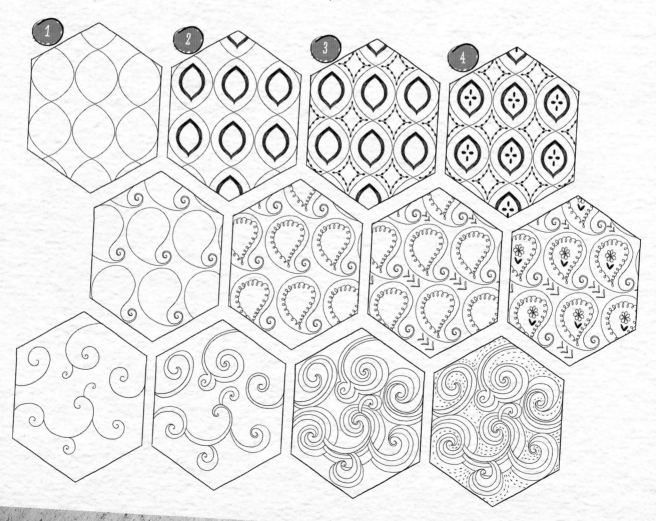

Original Letters

Picking the right letter style is key to crafting sensational lettering zendoodles. Take time to experiment with different looks, like the examples below. Or if you're feeling stuck, make letters that match a mood or adjective. Fill a page with playful, cool, classic, whimsical, and serious forms.

A A A A A

B B B B B

C C C C C

D D D D D

E E E E E

F F F f $\mathcal{F}$

G G G g $\mathcal{G}$

H H H $\mathcal{H}$ $\mathcal{H}$

I I I $\mathcal{J}$ $\mathcal{J}$

Types of Type

Typeface is a set of designed letters, characters, and symbols. There are hundreds of different types, but here are four main categories.

Serif: A common and classic typeface. Serif type has small lines, or serifs, on the ends of letters.

Sans Serif: Sans means "without." This type doesn't have serifs. Sans serif is considered a modern style.

Script: This typeface is based on handwriting. Script letters have a natural, flowing look.

Decorative: The showiest of all typefaces. Decorative types are designed to be unique and interesting.

Fabulous Filled Letters

Create a stunning letter by filling it up with an assortment of designs. Jam-pack your letters for a dense and intricate look. Or go open and airy for laid-back minimalism. Get inspired by nature and draw organic patterns or try happy swishes and squiggles. Just be sure to draw thick letters. That'll give you plenty of room to decorate with zendoodles.

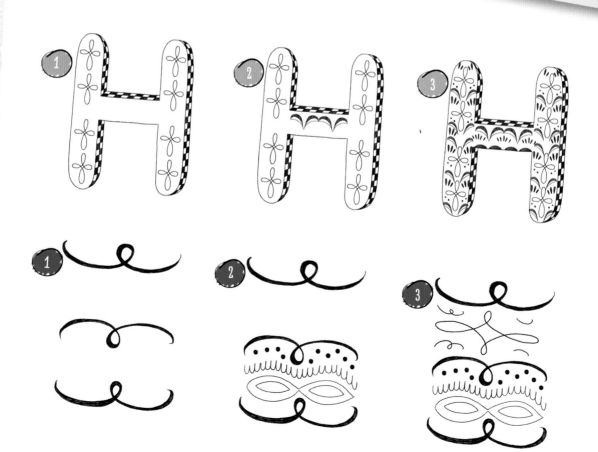

Sweet Trinkets & Charms

Accessorize your letters with dangle zendoodles. Build a chain of delicate shapes or draw a thin line with a charm at the end. Let the doodles hang gracefully from the letters. Try curly, wavy, and zigzagging lines for a new twist.

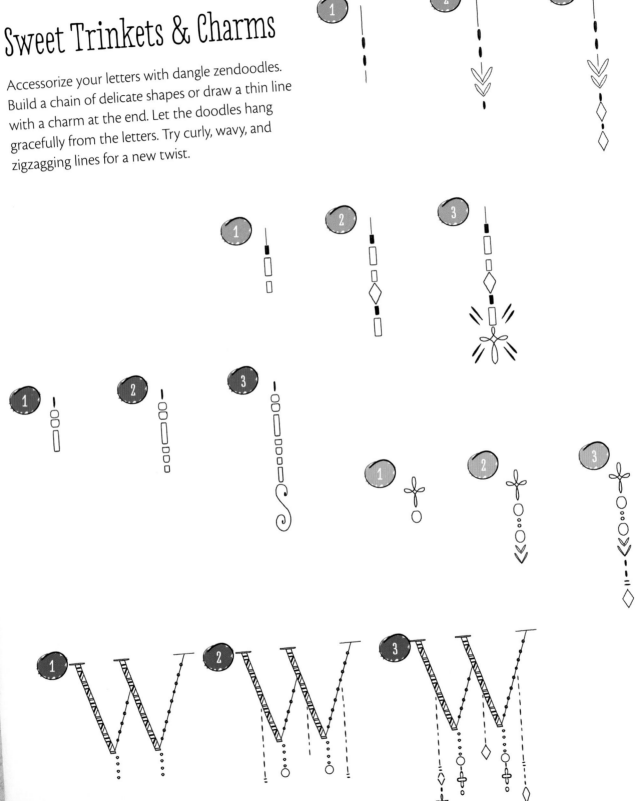

Charmed

Vertical doodles become extra sweet with a few additions. Draw a charm at the end of a dangle zendoodle to give it some weight and style. Experiment with the ones below or create charms that reflect your personality and interests.

Customized Monogram

Personalize the page with this chic monogram. Adorn the outside of your initials with lacy patterns. Finish the look by extending your doodles to form a shape. Circles are common, but go with whatever you like best. Try a star, diamond, or heart for a unique, eye-catching style.

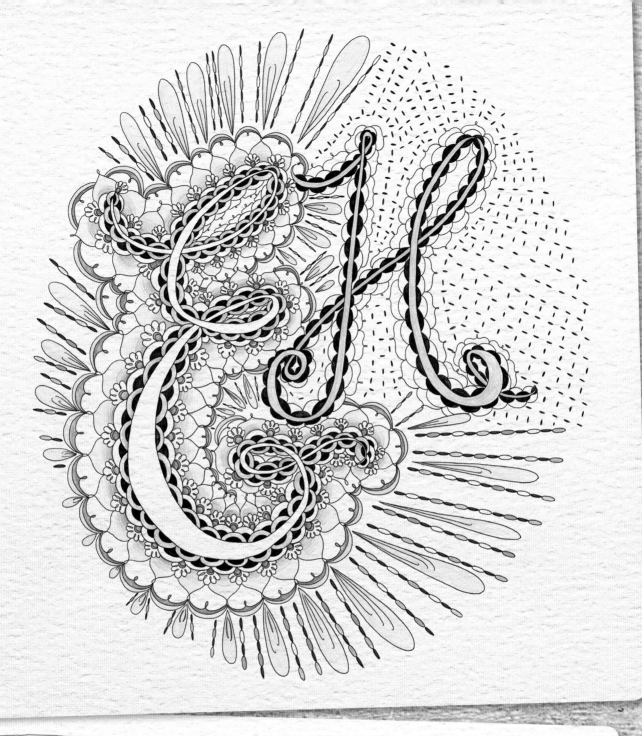

Tracing Type

Need help creating letters? Choose a font you like on the computer. Print it out at a big size, place it behind your drawing paper, and trace. If the drawing paper is too thick to see through, use a transfer technique. Take a pencil and completely cover the backside of the printed paper with graphite. Place the scribbled side facedown onto your drawing paper. Trace the letters. Your pencil will push the graphite into the other paper. Lift up the printed paper and use the transferred outlines to start your zendoodle!

Adorable A to Z

Put your imagination to the test! Unwind and create a zendoodle alphabet. Decorate thick letters with doodles or form letters out of tiny shapes. Go wild and make each letter different or keep a unifying element throughout. Whatever approach you use, it'll be uniquely you!

Striking Negative Space

Make your words pop with negative space. Begin by lightly drawing your letter or word. Draw everywhere except inside the letters. Try a free-for-all zendoodle. Or keep things neat and layer rows of patterns for an organized design.

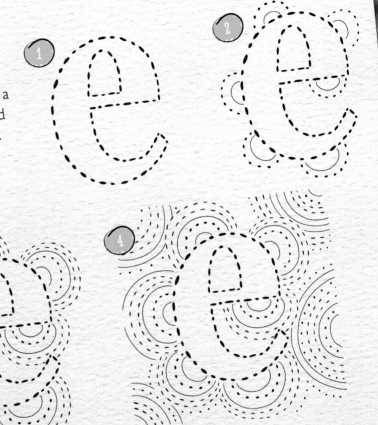

Creative Colored Pens

Freshen up your zendoodles and draw with colored pens! Switch out your black pen for bright neons, cool pastels, or sparkly glitter gel inks.

Here are a few ways to use your colored pens:

- Use one colored pen for the whole zendoodle.
- Pick a couple of colors. Doodle a large section in one color. Draw the next section in a new color. Alternate throughout the zendoodle.
- Draw the large shapes in your zendoodle using one color. Use other colors to make the patterns.
- Doodle in pen. Then take out colored pencils and color in your design. Choose hues similar to the pen for a coordinated look.

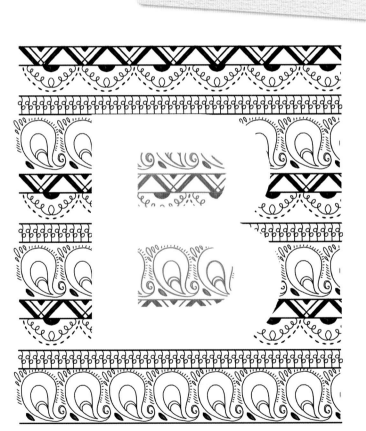

Embellished Hand Lettering

Add artsy attitude to a favorite word or motto. Style it with a mix of zendoodle flourishes. Work in related elements for harmonious look. You can always go abstract too. Try out a trendy angular pattern or flirty, curly design.

Enjoy your Journey

Sun

Sea

Zendoodles All Around

Bring some drama to your words. Embellish your name or a favorite word by surrounding it with fancy patterns. Add a few layers for a gentle accent. Or keep going until the whole page is covered in designs. Color the word to make it shine even more.

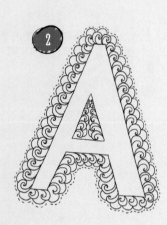

Swirly Cursive

Turn graceful script letters into works of art. Decorate with dashing doodle patterns. Then add extra swoops, curls, and other flourishes. Keep going until your design glows with effortless, twirly charm.

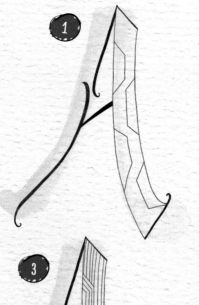

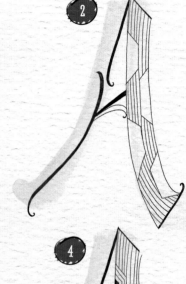

Adding Watercolor

For a soft splash of color, try watercolors. Start with thick drawing or watercolor paper. With a large brush, apply a thin layer of water to the page. Load your brush with watercolor and paint onto the wet paper. Create the general shape of your design or try an abstract form. Dry completely before doodling over it with pencil or pen.

Playing with Perspective

Lightly drawn guidelines make do-it-yourself word art easy. Create an expanding phrase by sketching two lines that flare away from each other. Letter between the lines. Have fun playing around with different guidelines. Try shaping, shrinking, and growing your letters!

1. BE BOLD

2. BE BOLD

3. BE BOLD

Oodles of Zendoodles

Don't just put doodles in your letters — *make* your words out of doodles! Sketch your letters first. Then start adding bubbly shapes, frilly lines, petals, and more. Use this twist to accent one letter or apply it to the whole word for a lush zendoodle.

Picture It!

Mesh words with images for a clever combination. Sketch the object first. Then stretch the letters so they fit inside the space. Or combine them with part of the image. Decorate any empty areas with doodles and details. Get creative with your pairings. See what cool mix you can design!

It's
TEAtimE

Motivational Mantra Art

Keep things positive with hand-lettered inspiration. Blend your go-to encouraging quote or saying with a pretty picture. Keep it small and focus on one image. Embellish it with a swirl of zendoodles. Or go big and design a whole scene. Add sweet doodle details to bring it all together.

Photo Fun

Bring a cool mixed-media look to your art. Instead of drawing a picture, use a photo to get your zendoodle started. Find an interesting image in your photographs. Or look online and in magazines. Carefully cut out the object and paste it onto your paper. Pair it with a favorite quote and embellish all around with doodles. It'll be picture perfect!

Keep Calm and plant poppies

Get Crafty!

Zendoodles don't have to stay in your sketchbook. These fancy doodles are perfect for decorating and adding flair to everyday items. All you need is a little creativity. So if you're feeling artsy, try a variety of projects and crafts that'll showcase your zendoodles to the world. Be inspired to create your own DIY masterpiece — take your zendoodles off the page!

VIP Mug

Create a functional and fashionable gift for a friend — or make one for yourself! Doodle onto a white mug using oil-based paint pens. Wipe off any mistakes with rubbing alcohol. When you're happy with the look, place your mug on a cookie sheet. Pop it into a cold oven. Heat the oven to 350 degrees F (180 degrees C) and bake for 30 minutes. Turn the oven off and leave the cup inside until it's completely cool. Hand wash your new mug to keep the decoration looking sharp.

Inspiring Canvas Art

Get ready to take on the world with upbeat artwork handcrafted by you. If you're confident with a paintbrush, use acrylic paint to beautify a plain canvas. Or use fabric or paint pens to make adding rows of tiny doodles a cinch. Keep the focus on your word and leave it white. It'll stand out against the colored zendoodle background.

ABCs Decor

This easy craft makes a bold statement. Pick up an oversized wood or cardboard letter at a craft store. Then doodle away with markers or paint pens. Customize it to coordinate with your bedroom's style. Try adding spots of glitter for extra glitz.

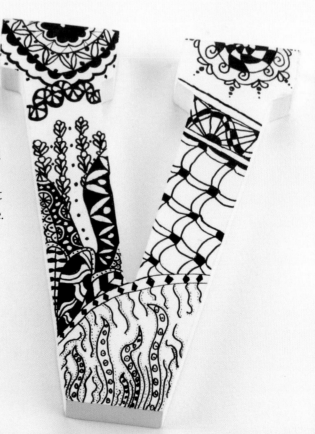

Dear Diary

Turn a bland notebook into your personal diary with darling zendoodles. Go with a brown cardboard cover for a casual, natural feel. Pair it with a design in black or white ink to keep it cool and fresh. Lightly draw your decoration in pencil first to get it just right.

Cute & Comfy Pillow

Snuggle up with your doodles! Fabric paint pens make it easy to design a custom textile. Just start with a plain pillowcase and make it your own. For a playful touch, try adding pom-poms. Sew on pom-pom trim or attach it with a bit of fabric glue. Chill out with your cozy creation.

DIY Thank You Card

Store-bought cards are fine in a hurry, but make your thank you extra meaningful with a handmade note. Decorate the card with a dramatic zendoodle design. Or keep it simple with a straightforward "thanks" embellished with a dainty doodle border. Make it a card to treasure forever!

Vintage Paper Zendoodles

Bring new life to old printed paper. Take a page from worn-out newspapers, magazines, or books and make it your doodle canvas. Free-flowing designs on top of orderly type combine for a unique, funky texture. Try letting a few meaningful words or phrases show through. Your upcycled art will be one of a kind.

Can't wait to draw your own zendoodles?

Visit **capstonekids.com** to download blank outlines. Simply print and start doodling. Add your own unique curls, twirls, and tangles!

Read More

Corfee, Stephanie. *Quirky, Cute Doodles*. Doodle with Attitude. North Mankato, Minn.: Capstone Press, 2016.

Marbaix, Jane. *Zentangle for Kids*. New York: Sterling Children's Books, 2015.

Warnaar, Dawn Nicole. *Adventures in Lettering: 40 Exercises to Improve Your Lettering Skills*. Lake Forest, Calif.: Walter Foster Jr., 2016.

Internet Sites

FactHound offers a safe, fun way to find Internet sites related to this book. All of the sites on FactHound have been researched by our staff.

Here's all you do:
Visit www.facthound.com
Type in this code: 9781515748410

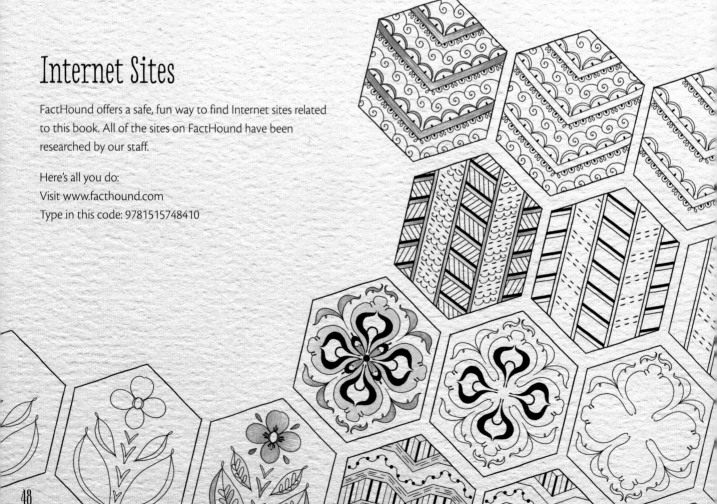